Original title:
Morning Trust

Copyright © 2025 Swan Charm
All rights reserved.

Author: Sabrina Sarvik
ISBN HARDBACK: 978-1-80560-243-9
ISBN PAPERBACK: 978-1-80560-708-3

Hope on the Horizon

In shadows deep where doubts do creep,
A whisper stirs, a promise to keep.
The dawn breaks clear, the night takes flight,
With every heart, a spark of light.

The road may twist, the path may bend,
Yet courage blooms with every friend.
Together we stand, hand in hand,
With dreams so bold, and futures planned.

When storms arise and skies turn gray,
We hold our breath, we find our way.
For in the rain, there lies a song,
A melody of hope, steadfast and strong.

Through valleys low and mountains high,
We chase the stars that fill the sky.
Each step we take, a tale unfurls,
Of faith and strength in this vast world.

So lift your gaze, let shadows wane,
For in our hearts, we break the chain.
A brighter day, it soon will gleam,
With hope on the horizon, we dare to dream.

Threads of Light

In the quiet dawn, they glimmer bright,
Weaving dreams in the soft morning light.
Each thread a promise, a whisper of hope,
Binding our hearts, helping us cope.

With every sunrise, they dance and sway,
Guiding our steps along the way.
Illuminating paths that we dare to tread,
In the tapestry of words that remain unsaid.

Blossoms of Trust

In gardens of silence, they bloom so rare,
Petals unfurl, delicate in air.
Each bloom a symbol, of faith we share,
Roots intertwined, beyond compare.

With gentle whispers, they sing a song,
Of unity found where we belong.
In the warmth of connection, we nurture and grow,
In the light of trust, our true selves show.

The Horizon's Embrace

Where earth meets sky, a promise unfolds,
In hues of amber, a story told.
The sun dips low, in a tender grace,
Cradling dreams in the horizon's embrace.

Waves of warmth wash over our souls,
As time stands still, and the heart extols.
With every sunset, a new dawn breaks,
In the quiet moment, our spirit wakes.

Softly Spoken Vows

In the still of night, vows softly shared,
Whispers of love, tender and bared.
Promises linger like stars in the sky,
Binding our hearts, you and I.

With each heartbeat, our spirits align,
In the dance of life, your hand in mine.
Through storms and silence, we'll find our way,
In softly spoken vows, forever we'll stay.

Threads of Day's Tapestry

In morning light, the shadows weave,
Colors dance, as hearts believe.
Each thread a story, softly spun,
Moments cherished, one by one.

The sun's warm embrace, a gentle breath,
Awakens dreams and whispers death.
A canvas bright where hopes align,
Through trials faced, our souls entwine.

In tangled paths of joy and pain,
We find our beauty, learn to gain.
With every choice, a pattern grows,
In the fabric of life, love always flows.

The gentle hum of life's sweet song,
Reminds us where we all belong.
In unity, our spirits rise,
Infinity waits beyond the skies.

As day unfolds, we weave anew,
With every dawn, a brighter view.
In this tapestry, bold and wide,
We find our peace, in time, our guide.

Dawn's Quiet Assurance

Morning slips through curtain folds,
A secret touch, the heart behold.
Softly whispers in the air,
Dawn's embrace, beyond compare.

The world awakes with gentle sighs,
As golden rays kiss sleepy eyes.
Promises made in every hue,
Assurance shines, so fresh and true.

Clouds drift softly, a tender show,
In tranquil moments, wisdom flows.
With each heartbeat, life ignites,
Guided forward by soft lights.

As shadows fade, the day unveils,
A wondrous tale that never pales.
The sun ascends, dispels the night,
In dawn's warm glow, there stands our light.

With hope renewed, our spirits soar,
In moments still, we yearn for more.
Dawn's quiet assurance sings,
Of brighter days and endless springs.

The Sun's Gentle Whisper

The sun breaks through the morning mist,
Its tender touch, a lover's kiss.
Across the sky, it spans the blue,
Whispers of warmth, a promise true.

Golden rays dance on the sea,
A symphony of what can be.
Nature's canvas, bright and bold,
Stories woven, yet untold.

Each sparkle glimmers, bright and rare,
A gentle call that beckons fair.
In every beam, we find our way,
Boundless hope in light of day.

With every whisper, fears subside,
In sunlight's glow, we stand with pride.
The world awakens, full of grace,
In the sun's arms, we find our place.

Embrace the warmth, let worries cease,
In tranquil moments, find your peace.
The sun's soft whisper calls us near,
With open hearts, we hold it dear.

Awakening to Possibility

The dawn arrives with open hands,
A symphony of life that stands.
Each moment swells with dreams unfurled,
A canvas bright, a brand new world.

We rise from slumber, spirits free,
Embracing all that we can be.
With every breath, we chase the light,
Awakening to endless might.

In gentle hues, the day unfolds,
New stories written, fate retold.
The future glimmers, wide and clear,
In every heartbeat, echoes sear.

Unlock the heart, let passions sing,
Within the dawn, our souls take wing.
Each second counts, a chance to grow,
In this vast dance, let courage flow.

Awakening to what may come,
With open hearts, we find our home.
As possibilities stretch and rise,
We chase the beauty in the skies.

Daylight's Embrace

The sun breaks through the foggy mist,
Awakening the world with bliss.
Golden rays kiss the morning dew,
A promise of the day that's new.

Birds sing sweetly in the trees,
Dancing softly in the breeze.
Colors burst, alive and bright,
In the warmth of daylight's light.

Fields of green, a vibrant hue,
Nature's canvas, fresh and true.
With each step, the heart feels free,
In this realm of tranquility.

Time slows down, the moment's pure,
In daylight's grasp, we feel secure.
A gentle call, a whisper kind,
Inviting us to leave behind.

Embrace the day, let worries fade,
In sunlight's glow, our fears betrayed.
For in this light, we find our way,
A path of hope, come what may.

Slumber's End

The moonlight fades, the stars retreat,
As dawn breaks softly, bittersweet.
In the stillness, dreams take flight,
A dance between the dark and light.

Whispers of night begin to wane,
As morning's breath clears the lane.
With every sigh, slumber departs,
Awakening the sleepy hearts.

Crisp air fills the waking space,
Light spills forth, a warm embrace.
The quiet hush of night is gone,
Replaced by day, where we move on.

Eyes flutter open, the world anew,
Each moment cherished, space to pursue.
With open arms, we greet the morn,
In the gentle light, our hopes are born.

So lay to rest the dreams once held,
In the light of day, be compelled.
For every end begets a start,
In slumber's end, we find our heart.

Breaths of New Light

Awakening beneath the sky,
Gentle whispers float on high.
Grass beneath our feet feels bright,
In the morning's tender light.

Fluttering leaves and petals bloom,
Filling the air with sweet perfume.
Chirps and laughter fill the day,
In the sun's warm, golden ray.

Hope arrives on this fresh dawn,
Inviting dreams to carry on.
Each breath we take, a gift anew,
In the light, our spirits grew.

Step by step, the journey flows,
With every sunrise, life bestows.
A canvas wide, with colors bright,
Painting paths in breaths of light.

So let us dance, embrace the day,
In harmony, we'll find our way.
For every moment, pure delight,
Awaits us in this new light.

The Day's Gentle Promise

With dawn's first glow, a promise made,
In soft hues that never fade.
The world awakens, fresh and bright,
In the arms of morning light.

Each moment bursts with hope and gleam,
Like flowing rivers, a vibrant stream.
Nature sings, in joyful tone,
A melody that's all our own.

The day unfolds, like petals wide,
With every step, we take in stride.
In its embrace, we find our place,
A journey rich with love and grace.

Let laughter rise, let sorrows bend,
In every heart, let joy descend.
For in this time, we live and dream,
In the gentle promise, we redeem.

So wander forth, with spirits high,
Beneath the vast, embracing sky.
For every dawn brings forth a chance,
To join in life's sweet, endless dance.

Glows of Trust

In whispers soft, we tread with care,
Words woven tight, like threads we share.
Through shadows deep, our hearts ignite,
In every glance, a spark of light.

Together we rise, come storm or shine,
With every pulse, our souls align.
In laughter's echo, and silence's hum,
A bond unbroken, forever to come.

With each embrace, our fears we shed,
In shared moments, new paths we tread.
Through trials faced and journeys long,
In trust we find where we belong.

A flicker bright in darkest night,
A beacon calling, guiding right.
Hand in hand, we face the dawn,
In glows of trust, we're never gone.

Morning's Soft Reassurance

As dawn breaks soft with hues of gold,
New dreams arise, their tales unfold.
The world awakes, in gentle grace,
With every sunbeam, a warm embrace.

The sky, a canvas painted bright,
Each ray a promise, pure delight.
In morning's glow, our worries fade,
In whispered hopes, a path is made.

Birds sing sweetly, a soothing song,
Reminding us where we belong.
With every breath, a chance is born,
In morning's light, we feel reborn.

So rise with joy, let shadows yield,
In this new day, our hearts will shield.
With faith that flows like rivers wide,
In morning's arms, we will confide.

The Promise of Tomorrow's Light

In twilight's hush, the stars confer,
A tapestry where dreams stir.
Each moment holds a chance anew,
A promise sealed with morning dew.

The night may bring its doubts and fears,
But dawn will wipe away the tears.
With every heartbeat, hope takes flight,
In the promise of tomorrow's light.

Clouds may gather, shadows play,
Yet through the storm, we find our way.
With open hearts, we seek our might,
In the promise of tomorrow's light.

As dawn unfurls its silken thread,
We rise again, no words unsaid.
In dreams we trust, our spirits bright,
For every day brings fresh delight.

A Day's Gentle Hope

With every dawn, a canvas new,
A chance to find what's pure and true.
In gentle winds, our worries sway,
As hope unfolds, a bright ballet.

Through petals soft, in gardens bloom,
We catch the whispers, dispel the gloom.
In laughter shared, and kindness shown,
A day's gentle hope has truly grown.

With every hug, and every smile,
We weave a dream, each precious mile.
In simple joys, we find our scope,
A testament to a day's hope.

So let us cherish every beat,
In quiet moments, where hearts meet.
For in this life, as rivers flow,
We'll carry on with gentle hope.

Beneath the Rising Sky

Beneath the rising sky, we stand,
With dreams and hopes in hand.
The horizon glows, a shimmering light,
As day embraces the night.

Soft whispers of the morning breeze,
Stir the leaves upon the trees.
Every shadow fades away,
Welcoming the promise of the day.

A canvas painted with hues of gold,
Stories of the brave and bold.
With each step, we claim our ground,
In this beauty, peace is found.

Birds take flight with joyful cries,
As sunlight spills across the sighs.
Together we chase the dawn anew,
With hearts aglow, the world feels true.

Beneath the rising sky, we dream,
In unity, we form a team.
For hope is born with every ray,
Guiding us along the way.

Faith in the Dawn

Faith in the dawn, a gentle spark,
Guiding our souls from cold to warm.
Through shadows thick, we find our path,
Embracing light, escaping wrath.

Each morning sings a melody,
Of possibility and destiny.
With arms wide open, we await,
The beauty that love can create.

Colors burst where dark once lay,
In the silence of the break of day.
We rise as one, our spirits free,
Believing in all we can be.

In every breath, a prayer ascends,
The world awakens, hope extends.
With faith in our hearts, we brightly glow,
Together we'll rise, together we'll grow.

Let the dawn bring forth its grace,
In every heart, find your place.
Faith in the dawn will light our way,
Transforming night's shadows to bright day.

Daybreak's Pledge

Daybreak's pledge, a promise made,
To chase the dark, let light invade.
With every sunbeam, hope will rise,
Casting away the night's disguise.

In the quiet of the morning's breath,
We gather strength beyond all death.
United in purpose, we will stand,
Together we forge a brighter land.

The dawn unfolds with softest glow,
A canvas where our dreams may flow.
With hearts that beat in rhythm true,
We embrace the day as a grand debut.

In gratitude, we lift our gaze,
To witness life's unfolding maze.
Daybreak's pledge is ours to keep,
Awakening truth from shadows deep.

With open hearts, we find our way,
In unity, we greet the day.
Daybreak's pledge, an oath we share,
To rise and shine, to love and care.

Serenity in the Sunrise

Serenity in the sunrise gleams,
Life awakens in golden dreams.
A tranquil moment to behold,
Whispers of warmth, stories untold.

The horizon blushes, colors blend,
Nature's symphony begins to mend.
In quietude, we find our peace,
As worries fade and fears release.

Beneath the canvas of soft light,
We gather strength, hearts warm and bright.
With every breath, let hope ignite,
In the embrace of the morning light.

As flowers bloom and birds take flight,
Life's rhythms dance in pure delight.
Serenity wraps the world anew,
A gentle promise in every hue.

In the stillness, we carve our dreams,
Bound by love, or so it seems.
Serenity in the sunrise stays,
Guiding us through the coming days.

Dawn's Gentle Whispers

Softly breaks the day anew,
Morning bathed in golden hue.
Birds begin their sweet refrain,
Nature stirs from nightly strain.

Waves of light on petals dance,
Every shadow has a chance.
Whispers float upon the air,
Promises beyond compare.

Clouds adorned in blushes bright,
Heralding the welcome light.
Every heartbeat, every sigh,
Awakens dreams that soar high.

Gentle breezes kiss the earth,
Celebrating the day's rebirth.
Horizon glows with warming grace,
In this tranquil, sacred space.

Dawn unfolds with quiet pride,
In her beauty, we confide.
Life begins anew each morn,
In the light, we are reborn.

Embrace of the Awakening Light

The sky ignites with shades of gold,
A tender tale of life retold.
Morning's breath, a soft caress,
In shadows past, now we express.

Trees stretch high, their branches sway,
Inviting warmth of the new day.
Each leaf glimmers, anew it sings,
Of joys that following light brings.

Illuminated paths we tread,
Following where the sun is led.
Radiance flows through every vein,
Erasing all remnants of pain.

Colors splash upon the scene,
Nature wakes, vibrant and keen.
Hope and peace in every sight,
We find solace in the light.

That gentle touch, that soft embrace,
Whispers of love in every place.
In this dance of day and night,
We rejoice in awakening light.

In the Arms of the Rising Sun

Crimson rays touch the tranquil sea,
In the arms of day, we're free.
Waves of warmth, a soft allure,
A moment's peace, forever pure.

Mountains glow in morning's light,
Every peak a thrilling sight.
The world awakens, fresh and bright,
Held gently in the sun's warm might.

Tender beams embrace the land,
With every heartbeat, hope is fanned.
In this haven, dreams take flight,
Souls align with the rising light.

Birds take wing, their spirits soar,
In harmony, they sing of more.
The sun bestows its radiant kiss,
In its embrace, we find our bliss.

Each dawn brings a chance to start,
A canvas bright for every heart.
In the sun's arms, we belong,
Finding strength, we rise as strong.

Promises Carried by the Breeze

Whispers ride on gentle air,
Promises linger everywhere.
In every rustle, hope we find,
Dancing lightly, intertwined.

Leaves flutter under skies so wide,
Nature's breath, our hearts confide.
Carried forth on wings of grace,
Each soft sigh, a warm embrace.

In the gardens where dreams bloom,
Breezes sweep away the gloom.
Every petal, every seed,
Carved in love, fulfilling need.

As twilight weaves its golden thread,
The world whispers of dreams ahead.
In every gust, our hopes arise,
The breeze carries our silent cries.

In the dance of day and night,
Promises float, a pure delight.
On the winds, our spirits glide,
Together, we embrace the ride.

The Sun's Silent Oath

In the dawn's embrace, soft and warm,
Promises whispered, nature's charm.
Shadows retreat, darkness fades,
Life awakens as light invades.

Each ray a vow, pure and bright,
Guiding the day with gentle light.
Golden hues paint the skies,
In the silence, hope always lies.

The sun will rise, that it's sure,
Bringing forth what hearts endure.
A constant presence, ever bold,
In its warmth, stories unfold.

Moments captured in a glance,
Nature's rhythm, a sacred dance.
Together, we thrive, we grow,
Under the sun's eternal glow.

As dusk descends, a soft sigh,
The sun bows low, bids goodbye.
Yet in our hearts, its truth stays,
In whispered oaths, the sun displays.

Balancing on Day's Edge

When twilight treads the border line,
Shadows lengthen, stars align.
Nature holds its breath to see,
The balance of night, the day's decree.

Colors shift in brilliant hues,
Merging skies with tender views.
On this edge, time feels still,
An aching calm, a gentle thrill.

The whispers of wind softly call,
Echoing dreams where shadows fall.
Moments flicker like fireflies,
In the dusk, truth never lies.

With courage built on fleeting light,
We dance between day and night.
Each heartbeat marks the time that's near,
Embracing change without the fear.

On this precipice, we find our way,
Guided by the light of day.
Balancing between dark and bright,
In the stillness, we ignite.

The Heart of Awakening Light

Softly breaks the morning glow,
A symphony of life below.
In shadows long, the sun does rise,
Awakens dreams beneath the skies.

Hope ignites in the lingering dark,
A flicker here, a vibrant spark.
With every pulse, the earth feels right,
Breathing deep the dawning light.

Waves of warmth cascade and flow,
Unfolding petals, nature's show.
In the heart of each new day,
Miracles whisper, come what may.

Filling spaces once forlorn,
With colors bright as dreams are born.
The heart beats strong, the world spins free,
In the light, we find our key.

As sunlight dances on the ground,
A symphony of life resounds.
Awakening within our sight,
Hope resides in every light.

Emanations of Faith

In quiet moments, faith takes flight,
Soft whispers echo in the night.
Emotions rise like morning mist,
In the heart where dreams exist.

Through trials faced, we find our way,
Guided by light of hope's array.
Each prayer a beacon, shining bright,
Lighting paths through shadows' plight.

Together we stand, hand in hand,
Energized by a steadfast band.
Trust in the journey, step by step,
In this bond, our spirit's kept.

Messages carried on the breeze,
Whispers of love that aim to please.
With every heartbeat, we embrace,
The beauty found in faith's grace.

Emanations swirl, bright and bold,
Stories of courage, quietly told.
In the dance of life, we sway,
The light of faith guides our way.

Chorus of New Beginnings

In the dawn of day, we rise,
Hope ignites, a bright surprise.
With every step, a story starts,
New dreams whisper in our hearts.

The past is gone, a distant sound,
In the present, joy is found.
With open arms, we greet the chance,
To weave our lives in a daring dance.

Each moment flows like gentle streams,
Carrying forth our woven dreams.
With courage in our hearts so true,
We chase the skies, we paint them blue.

Together here, we stand as one,
Underneath the warm, golden sun.
With every voice, a harmony,
In this chorus, we are free.

So let us rise, let laughter soar,
Embrace the new, forevermore.
In unity, we find our way,
This chorus sings of a brand new day.

Radiance and Reverie

In twilight's glow, where dreams take flight,
A dance of stars breaks the night.
Whispers soft as the evening breeze,
Carried through the rustling trees.

Moonlit paths reveal the lore,
Of timeless tales that linger more.
With every glance, a secret shared,
In silence deep, our spirits bared.

The heart's embrace, a tender glow,
In radiance, we come to know.
These fleeting moments, bright and rare,
Are memories that linger in the air.

Through reverie's lens, we dare to dream,
In shadows cast by the silver beam.
With eyes wide open, we seek the light,
In dreams awakened, we take flight.

Together here, beneath the sky,
In harmony, we'll learn to fly.
With every heartbeat, love will grow,
In this radiance, forever flow.

First Light's Assurance

The dawn awakens with a song,
Promises of hope where we belong.
In the stillness, whispers rise,
As sunlight dances, painting skies.

Each ray a brush on canvas bright,
Guiding hearts from dark to light.
With every step, we find our way,
Through shadows cast, into the day.

The warmth unfolds in soft embrace,
In first light's glow, we find our place.
With gentle courage, we will stand,
United here, together hand in hand.

The path ahead may twist and turn,
In every challenge, strength we learn.
With open hearts, we face the morn,
In first light's arms, new dreams are born.

So let us cherish this embrace,
In every moment, each trace.
With hope renewed, we journey on,
In first light's promise, we're never alone.

A Gentle Brush of Gold

As day unfolds in hues so bright,
A gentle brush of gold ignites.
The world awakens, soft and clear,
In every heartbeat, love draws near.

Fields of amber swaying low,
Whispers carry on the wind's soft flow.
Nature's symphony in sweet refrain,
A tranquil peace amidst the gain.

With every dawn, a chance to see,
The beauty in simplicity.
Each moment's grace, a precious gift,
In gentle waves, our spirits lift.

The sun's warm kiss upon our face,
Is a reminder of this sacred space.
In laughter shared, we find our way,
Through gentle brushstrokes of the day.

So let us cherish every hue,
In life's vast canvas, old and new.
With hearts aligned, we'll never fold,
In this embrace, our dreams of gold.

Dawn's Embrace

In the hush of the morning light,
Softly the shadows take flight.
Colors bloom like flowers' grace,
Everything stirs in dawn's embrace.

Whispers dance on the cool air,
Dreams linger with gentle care.
A symphony of golden rays,
Awakens the world in dazzling ways.

Birds sing sweet songs from the trees,
Heartfelt echoes ride the breeze.
Nature's canvas begins to sing,
As the day unfolds its wings.

Light spills over the hills' crest,
Painting the sky, a vibrant fest.
Every moment, a fleeting spark,
Embracing the warmth as it embarks.

In this dance of light and shade,
Life's new stories are displayed.
Dawn's embrace, a tender kiss,
A promise of a day full of bliss.

Whispered Promises of Daylight

As dawn breathes softly in shades of gold,
Stories of night begin to unfold.
Whispered promises linger and sway,
Inviting the heart to embrace the day.

Mist drifts softly, gentle and shy,
Under the canvas of the waking sky.
With each ray, shadows fade away,
Unveiling the beauty of a brand new day.

Rippling waters catch the sun's glow,
Reflecting the dreams we long to know.
Each moment, a treasure we hold dear,
Daylight's whispers beckon us near.

Fields awaken, dressed in dew's grace,
Every blade of grass finds its place.
In the warmth of the sun's embrace,
Life unfolds in a tender pace.

With every heartbeat, a song is sung,
In the light of day, hopes are sprung.
Whispers guide us, gentle, bold,
Through whispered promises, life unfolds.

Let the daylight warm the soul's hue,
In the dance of time, we renew.
With each dawn, a fresh start awaits,
In whispered promises, love creates.

The Awakening Canvas

Morning breaks on the horizon wide,
A canvas painted with colors that glide.
Brushstrokes of light in a vibrant race,
Creating beauty with every embrace.

Mountains stand tall, kissed by the sun,
As nature stirs, a new day's begun.
With every hue, the world ignites,
Awakening softly in soft daylight.

Blossoms unfold in fragrant delight,
As the canvas of dreams takes flight.
With petals bright against a clear sky,
In this moment, our spirits will fly.

Clouds drift slowly, a painter's brush,
Crafting shadows, creating a hush.
In this quiet, the heart sings loud,
Within the grace, we feel so proud.

Every drop of dew, a tiny world,
Beneath the sun's touch, gently twirled.
As we stand here, time slips away,
In the awakening canvas of the day.

Colors blend in a harmonious wave,
In this moment, we feel so brave.
Life's masterpiece, a joy to see,
On this canvas, we're truly free.

Sunlit Bonds

Beneath the sun's warm, golden gaze,
Hearts entwined in a joyful haze.
Promises whispered in each gentle breeze,
Creating bonds that time shall seize.

Through fields of gold, we dance and play,
Hand in hand, come what may.
With laughter echoing wide and far,
In the embrace of the shining star.

As shadows stretch and daylight gleams,
We weave together our shared dreams.
In every moment, a story unfolds,
In sunlit bonds, our love upholds.

Time slows down in the sunlit glow,
Where joy and peace seem to overflow.
With every heartbeat, the world feels right,
In sunlit bonds, we shine so bright.

Seasons change, but our roots run deep,
Nurtured by memories, ours to keep.
In the warmth of the sun, we find our way,
In countless moments of a golden day.

Together we stand through thick and thin,
Bound by the love that lies within.
In sunlit bonds, our journey flows,
Forever cherished, as life bestows.

Serenity in Sunlight

Golden rays kiss the dawn,
Whispers of peace in the air.
Leaves dance in the soft breeze,
Moments of stillness, so rare.

Nature hums a gentle tune,
Hearts open wide to the light.
In the calm, we find ourselves,
Everything feels pure and right.

Shadows fade as warmth unfolds,
Casting doubts into the past.
With each breath, harmony glows,
In this embrace, we are amassed.

Sunbeams weave through the trees,
Touching souls with tender grace.
In this sacred time and space,
Serenity finds its place.

With each step, joy's echo lingers,
A dance of heartbeats in time.
Here's to peace in life's embrace,
In sunlight, we find our rhyme.

Glimmers of a New Path

Dewdrops sparkle on the grass,
Morning light breaks through the haze.
Each step unveils the unknown,
Signposts guide in subtle ways.

Whispers carry dreams untold,
Hope ignites with every breath.
In the journey, hearts unfold,
Drawing strength from love, not death.

Footprints lead to pastures bright,
Where the wildflowers bloom anew.
Every choice a chance to grow,
Embracing change, we find what's true.

Horizons stretch beyond the now,
Bridges form from faith and trust.
With the dawn of endless dreams,
We step forward, rise from dust.

Life's a tapestry we weave,
Threads of light in every seam.
New paths call with gentle voices,
Awake to love, awake to dream.

Faith's Arrival at Day's Gate

When shadows retreat from the light,
Faith arrives like the morning sun.
Every fear begins to take flight,
In the warmth, we find we've won.

Golden rays touch weary souls,
Hope ignites in hearts once cold.
With each dawn, new strength unfolds,
In this moment, stories told.

Promises dance on the breeze,
Glistening with the dew of truth.
In the hush, our worries cease,
Renewed by the joy of youth.

Step by step towards the bright,
Guided by trust's gentle hand.
Here at the gate of the light,
Faith leads us to promise land.

In every heart, a small flame,
Burning fiercely, never dim.
At day's gate, we call its name,
In faith, we find life's sweet hymn.

Awakening Journeys

In twilight's embrace, we arise,
Hearts ignited, dreams in flight.
With every step, new wisdom lies,
Guided by stars, we chase the light.

Across valleys, through the stone,
Nature speaks in vibrant tones.
Each mountain climbed, we find our own,
In the silence, wisdom roams.

Tales of journeys intertwine,
Threads of courage weave our fate.
Embrace the path, let spirits shine,
In this dance, we cultivate.

The horizon calls our names,
Echoing in the evening breeze.
In the journey, nothing's the same,
Embracing change with hearts at ease.

Tomorrows stretch like endless skies,
With every dawn, new wings take flight.
Awakening journeys, bold replies,
Together, we step into the light.

Celestial Awakening

In the hush of the night sky,
Stars begin their gentle dance.
Whispers of dreams float by,
Guiding us to a waking trance.

The moon casts a silver glow,
Painting paths on silent seas.
With every heartbeat, we know,
A new dawn calls us to seize.

Birds stir in their hidden nests,
Nature's lullaby sings clear.
The world sheds its quiet rests,
Preparing for the day to cheer.

Colors blush as twilight fades,
Gold and orange brush the blue.
A symphony of light cascades,
Revealing skies with endless hue.

Awakening the soul's deep sighs,
Breath of life in morning's kiss.
Celestial patterns in our eyes,
Every sunrise brings pure bliss.

Sun Greets the Horizon

The sun peeks over hills so high,
Spilling warmth on sleepy ground.
Kissing clouds in the brightening sky,
With golden rays, joy is found.

Birds take flight on the fresh morning breeze,
Chirping tunes of a brand new day.
Nature's light through the dancing trees,
Welcomes all in a vibrant display.

Shadows retreat with the dawn's embrace,
Illuminating every hidden shape.
Life awakens to the sun's warm trace,
Sketching pathways where dreams escape.

Colorful blossoms stretch and yawn,
Unfurling petals to greet the light.
Their fragrance lingers till the dawn,
Painting the garden with pure delight.

The sun reigns high in the azure dome,
Chasing night into distant lore.
With each ray, it calls us home,
Encouraging hearts to soar.

A New Chapter Unfolds

Turn the page, let the tale begin,
Whispers of hope dance on the breeze.
With ink of courage, let dreams spin,
A journey awaits, sown with ease.

Hearts beat fast as the story starts,
Paths diverge in the morning light.
Every ending is a work of art,
Crafting futures that feel so bright.

Let go of doubt, embrace the unknown,
Each moment a thread of fate.
With every step, confidence grown,
A new chapter, we eagerly await.

The canvas blank, waiting for hues,
Brush in hand, unleash your spark.
With every stroke, there's so much to choose,
Creating beauty from the dark.

Embrace the dawn of fresh desires,
Let passions guide where dreams will lead.
With open hearts and burning fires,
Write the story of your own seed.

Daylight's Tender Greetings

As day breaks with gentle cheer,
Sunlight spills on dewy grass.
Nature whispers, "I am here,"
Inviting joys that come to pass.

Each leaf glistens with morning's tears,
An orchestra of light and sound.
Awakening all our hidden fears,
Revealing wonder all around.

The world hums softly, breathing deep,
In rhythms only dawn can bring.
Awaking dreams from their silent sleep,
As birds begin their songs to sing.

Every moment holds a promise bright,
In the heart of this new day.
Embrace the warmth, let go of night,
Feel the magic drift and sway.

Daylight ushers in tender grace,
With each ray, a moment to hold.
Every face, a smiling trace,
A new story waiting, yet untold.

The First Breath of Day

A gentle whisper through the trees,
The sun peeks shyly, warming seas.
Birds awaken, sing their song,
Embracing light where nights belong.

The dew glistens on blades of grass,
Each droplet holds the moments passed.
A canvas laid of gold and blue,
As shadows fade, the day feels new.

Dreams dissolve with morning's light,
Soft hues paint the sky so bright.
A world transforms, reborn anew,
In every heart, a spark breaks through.

Mountains rise, embracing the dawn,
With colors bold, the dark is gone.
Through every corner, life awakes,
In each breath, the future breaks.

Hold close this gift, the day has brought,
A tapestry of hope, intertwined and sought.
With open hearts, we take our flight,
In the first breath of day, we find our light.

Silhouettes of Hope at Daybreak

Silhouettes dance in morning's glow,
Promises blooming where shadows flow.
Every figure tells a tale,
Of dreams unfolding, passions strong and pale.

The horizon blushes, a soft embrace,
As light spills gently, erasing space.
In every shape, a story we see,
Of paths untraveled, of what could be.

Whispers linger in the breeze,
Carried with the rustling leaves.
Each step forward, a leap of faith,
As dawn's sweet chorus fills the wraith.

Embracing change, we rise anew,
With every heartbeat, hope rings true.
The silhouettes, a guide to trust,
In the light of day, we change, we must.

As sunbeams break the chains of night,
Together, we journey toward the light.
With open eyes, we face the day,
And let our spirits lead the way.

Caresses of a New Beginning

The morning's touch, soft as a sigh,
Embraces dreams that dare to fly.
With every heartbeat, the world unfolds,
In whispers of hope that it gently holds.

A canvas blank, a chance to write,
Stories woven in morning light.
Every step taken, a dance of grace,
In the arms of time, we find our place.

Breath of the dawn, so pure, so clear,
Erases the shadows, dispels all fear.
A promise shines in each sunrise,
For every ending, a new surprise.

The path ahead is yet untraced,
Each moment savored, each joy embraced.
With heart wide open, we face the day,
Guided by love that won't sway.

In caresses soft, the future gleams,
Carried forth on waves of dreams.
Every heartbeat marks a new start,
In this symphony, we play our part.

The Light's Tender Assurance

When shadows stretch and doubts arise,
A beacon glows across the skies.
The light, a friend, with hand outstretched,
Promises hope, forever etched.

With every dawn, the past releases,
Restoring faith, the heart eases.
A quiet warmth, a soothing balm,
Reminds us always we are calm.

In gentle hues of amber gold,
A story of resilience unfolds.
For every trial, the light persists,
A guiding star that surely exists.

Embrace the warmth, let worries fade,
In the glow of day, foundations laid.
With light as compass, we explore,
Together, we seek, together, we soar.

The tender assurance that life provides,
In every moment where love resides.
In the warmth of light, our spirits sing,
Together united, in joy we bring.

Between Night's Fading Echoes

In twilight's grasp, shadows dance,
Whispers linger, a fleeting chance.
Stars begin to melt away,
As dawn breaks in a soft display.

Gentle tides of night retreat,
Heartbeats sync with dawn's heartbeat.
The moon's glow dims, a brief farewell,
As daylight wakes, stories to tell.

The breeze carries secrets anew,
Life awakens, a vibrant hue.
Colors stretch across the sky,
Promises as the night says goodbye.

Between the stars and morning light,
Lies a tale of dark and bright.
Awake in dreams, we find our way,
Embracing hope in the light of day.

In every echo, night departs,
Filling dawn with hopeful hearts.
With every breath, a chance to see,
The beauty born of harmony.

Sunlit Bonds of Awakening

Golden rays break through the trees,
Nature stirs with waking ease.
Grass beneath our toes, so warm,
In sunlit fields, we find our form.

The world ignites with vibrant hues,
Whispers of life in every muse.
Birds take flight, their songs the air,
In joyous notes, we shed our care.

Hand in hand, we chase the light,
Guided by the sun's delight.
In laughter shared, our spirits soar,
Boundless love forevermore.

Butterflies flit from bloom to bloom,
While flowers dance, dispelling gloom.
In every heartbeat, nature's call,
Together we rise, together we fall.

In this moment, all is clear,
Our dreams awakened, held so near.
With every breath, we find our place,
In the sunlit bonds of warm embrace.

Trusting in Nature's Rhythm

The river flows with timeless grace,
In its song, we find our pace.
Mountains stand, steadfast and true,
Nature's heartbeat, pure and blue.

Leaves flutter softly in the breeze,
Whispers weaving through the trees.
Each step taken, a dance renewed,
In harmony, our souls imbued.

The sun will rise, the moon will wane,
Cycles of life, joy, and pain.
In every season, lessons learned,
Through faith in nature, hope is turned.

Trusting tides will guide our way,
Through shadows cast at end of day.
With every dawn, a chance to mend,
In nature's arms, we find a friend.

Rhythms pulse in every heart,
A symphony, nature's art.
Together we sing, our spirits free,
Embracing life's sweet harmony.

Echoes of Yesterday's Dreams

In twilight's depth, whispers call,
Echoes linger, shadows fall.
Memories dance, soft and bright,
Carried on the wings of night.

Through the mist, past journeys flow,
Dreams once lost, now begin to glow.
Fleeting moments, a tender trace,
In the heart's depths, a sacred space.

Old reflections in the mirror,
Tales of love that grow much dearer.
The past, a canvas softly drawn,
Painted shades of dusk till dawn.

With every heartbeat, truths align,
Silhouettes of what was mine.
Beneath the stars, I hold them near,
The echoes whisper, crystal clear.

In dreams, the past embraces now,
In every sigh, a promise, a vow.
Echoes of time, forever gleam,
In the quiet, we find a dream.

Embraced by Radiance

In the dawn's gentle glow,
Whispers of warmth arise.
Hues of gold stretch and flow,
Kissing the sleep from my eyes.

Clouds part like ancient scrolls,
Secrets of light unfurled.
Radiance fills my soul,
Waking a dreaming world.

Every shadow retreats,
Chased by the morning sun.
Life rhythmically beats,
Each day has just begun.

Nature so sweetly sings,
Branches dance in the breeze.
Hope in each moment brings,
A symphony to please.

Hand in hand with chance,
Together we shall stride.
In this bright expanse,
No need to hide or bide.

The Early Light's Faith

Softly the dawn paints the sky,
With colors fresh and bright.
Promises whispered nearby,
In the stillness of light.

The world begins to awake,
As dew glimmers like stars.
Each moment we softly take,
Turns dreams into memoirs.

Birds sing their morning song,
Notes dance on gentle air.
In this place we belong,
With faith, we rise and care.

Golden rays pierce the dark,
Guiding through every fear.
Each day a brand new spark,
With love drawing us near.

We walk under wide skies,
Threads of hope intertwine.
In the dawn, freedom flies,
A destiny divine.

Blossoming Day

Morning breaks with a smile,
Blossoms wake from their sleep.
In each fleeting while,
A promise we shall keep.

Colors burst forth anew,
Petals greet the first light.
In this vibrant view,
All shadows take to flight.

The breeze brings sweet perfume,
Nature hums her own tune.
Underneath the bright bloom,
We feel the sun's warm boon.

Every heartbeat a chance,
To dance in joyful sway.
In this life's lovely dance,
We blossom, come what may.

With each step we create,
A garden rich and vast.
In love, we celebrate,
All moments unsurpassed.

Hues of Hope at Daybreak

Silhouettes of dreams rest,
In the hush of night's end.
As day breaks with its quest,
New horizons to blend.

Brushstrokes of pastel skies,
Ink the canvas of dawn.
Painting life as it flies,
With each moment reborn.

Through the mist, hope appears,
Soft light touching the trees.
Washing away all fears,
A gentle morning breeze.

In this moment so rare,
We find strength in our hearts.
With love's tender care,
We embrace fresh new starts.

The tapestry unfolds,
With threads of dreams and light.
In hues, our spirit holds,
A promise shining bright.

The Ballet of Light

In the dawn, soft rays play,
Dancing dreams twirl and sway.
Whispers of hope in the air,
Gentle movements everywhere.

Colors burst in painted skies,
Nature's symphony never lies.
Every beam a story told,
In the warmth, we feel consoled.

Light caresses the morning dew,
Embracing life in shades anew.
With each step, shadows retreat,
In this ballet, love's heartbeat.

The sun ascends, commanding grace,
A golden touch on every face.
Awake, the world in pure delight,
Lost in the ballet of light.

Promises in the East

As daylight breaks, colors rise,
Painting dreams across the skies.
Whispers of dawn in the breeze,
Nature's promise, hearts at ease.

In the silence of a new day,
Hope awakens, shadows sway.
Golden rays of warmth extend,
A bright beginning, time to mend.

Every star that fades from view,
Carries stories, old and new.
In the east, a light bestowed,
Guiding paths on destinies road.

Softly spoken, dreams take flight,
In the promise of morning light.
Echoes of faith fill the air,
With each sunrise, life we share.

Shadows Fade with Faith

In the twilight, whispers blend,
Where the dark and light transcend.
Holding hands, we stand as one,
Facing fears till fears are done.

Shadows creep, but hearts grow bold,
In our unity, warmth unfolds.
Through the night, we find our way,
With each step, doubts drift away.

Faith like lanterns lights the path,
In its glow, we find our wrath.
Every teardrop turned to grace,
With hope's embrace, we find our place.

Step by step, as shadows fade,
In the light, our fears dismayed.
Together strong, we brave the storm,
With faith as guide, our spirits warm.

A New Day's Story

Each sunrise brings a tale untold,
With every ray, a new dawn unfolds.
Moments crafted by time's own hand,
Gifted to us, a brightening land.

In the silence, possibilities bloom,
Painting life in every room.
A canvas stretched, colors collide,
In the heart where dreams abide.

Voices rise with the morning song,
Telling of where we all belong.
Every heartbeat, a rhythmic cheer,
In the promise of a day sincere.

As daylight pours from heights above,
We weave our tales, filled with love.
With each glance at the sky so blue,
Through joy and trial, we start anew.

The Canvas of a Fresh Start

Each dawn unfurls a vibrant hue,
Washing away the night's despair.
With every brush, dreams come to view,
Hope paints a world beyond compare.

Old burdens lift with morning's ray,
As colors blend and overlap.
In this moment, come what may,
Life's masterpiece unfolds, no gap.

A palette filled with courage bright,
Each stroke a whisper of the soul.
In the silence, find your light,
Fragments unite to make you whole.

The canvas waits for hearts to dare,
To write their stories, bold and true.
In every stroke, a breath of air,
The art of life begins anew.

When Shadows Surrender to Light

In twilight's dance, the shadows play,
Fading echoes of the past.
With every moment, night gives way,
As dawn arrives, its colors cast.

Whispers linger in the breeze,
But light commands the dark to yield.
Silent sorrows start to cease,
In warming rays, our hearts are healed.

The quiet strength of life's embrace,
Chases fears into the void.
We find ourselves in the space,
Where light and hope are both employed.

With every step, we rise and grow,
As shadows melt from day to day.
A brighter path begins to show,
When darkness gives its final sway.

Illumination of Serene Possibilities

In the stillness, dreams arise,
A soft glow speaks of what can be.
Beneath the vast and endless skies,
Every thought becomes a key.

Whispers of hope float on the air,
Guiding hearts to places bright.
With belief, we dare to share,
The gifts of endless pure delight.

As moments bloom like flowers rare,
Each petal holds a hidden truth.
In quiet breaths, we find our care,
The scent of love returns our youth.

The horizon shimmers with desire,
A canvas drawn with dreams untold.
In every heart, a blazing fire,
Illuminates the brave and bold.

A Symphony of Daylight's Embrace

The morning sings a soft refrain,
Each note a promise to behold.
With sunlight dripping like sweet rain,
The world awakens, bright and bold.

A harmony of joy unfolds,
As nature whispers tunes of grace.
In every leaf, a tale retold,
In every smile, a warm embrace.

The wind joins in, a gentle guide,
Carrying laughter through the trees.
With each heartbeat, doubts subside,
In daylight's arms, we find our ease.

Let every moment be a song,
In unity, our spirits soar.
In daylight's glow, we all belong,
Together weaving evermore.

Faith Wrapped in Sunbeams

In the morning light we rise,
Where hope ignites the skies.
Every shadow fades away,
Chasing doubts that led astray.

Golden rays on weary hearts,
Softly heal our broken parts.
With each beam, a promise made,
A new beginning, unafraid.

In the whispers of the trees,
Lies a longing, sweet like bees.
Nature sings of trust and grace,
In this warm and sacred space.

Harvest dreams, the fields await,
Open arms, we celebrate.
Together in this radiant glow,
Faith blooms bright, in hearts we sow.

Sunset glimmers, day takes flight,
In the dusk, our spirits light.
Wrapped in warmth, we stand as one,
Faith renewed, beneath the sun.

Lullabies of the Dawn

Whispers float on morning air,
Softly, gently, without a care.
Dreams may fade as shadows fade,
In the dawn, new songs are made.

Crimson skies and golden streams,
Awake the world from silent dreams.
Every note a sweet embrace,
In this tranquil, glowing space.

Birds begin their morning tune,
Echoes dance beneath the moon.
Lullabies of light inspire,
Kindling hearts with gentle fire.

Past the night, our visions soar,
Opening each and every door.
Find your peace within the sound,
As the love of dawn surrounds.

Let the sun kiss every face,
Fill the heart with joy and grace.
In these moments, soft and tender,
Lullabies, we will remember.

Starry Farewells

As the day gives its last glow,
Stars awaken, soft and slow.
Whispers echo in the night,
Sending dreams on wings of light.

Farewell to the sun's warm rays,
Embrace the night in quiet ways.
Each twinkle tells a tale of old,
Mysteries of the night unfold.

Casting shadows, moonlight gleams,
Guiding paths for wanderers' dreams.
In this canvas, dark and vast,
We find solace in the past.

Stars that shine with timeless grace,
Illuminate this sacred space.
In the stillness, hearts take flight,
Facing both the dark and light.

Hold these moments, soft and bright,
In the realm where dreams ignite.
Starry farewells, memories stay,
Lighting futures, come what may.

Skylight Serenade

Through the window, bright and clear,
Melodies of life, we hear.
Skylight beams on heart and soul,
Filling pieces, making whole.

Every note a breath of peace,
In this harmony, fears release.
Chasing worries, one by one,
In this serenade, we run.

Gentle music in the skies,
Lifts our spirits, makes us rise.
Skyward glances, dreams take flight,
In the day as well as night.

Clouds may dance and winds may sigh,
Yet the song will never die.
Through the trials, through the pain,
Hope returns, like soft spring rain.

In the chords that touch the heart,
Where the world and dreams impart.
Skylight serenades our being,
In each moment, love is freeing.

The Morning Ray's Gentle Caress

The sun spills gold upon the ground,
Whispers of warmth, a soft surround.
Feathered songs in gentle flight,
Usher in the day from night.

Plants stretch wide, their leaves unfold,
Nurtured by the sun's soft gold.
Shadows fade as light prevails,
In every heart, a joy unveils.

Beams dance lightly on dew-kissed grass,
Nature's symphony as morning comes to pass.
With every ray, hope's flame ignites,
A world awakened, pure delights.

Across the sky, colors blend and play,
The dawn's embrace, a bright ballet.
In this moment, dreams take flight,
Boundless joy emerges from the night.

As day begins, our spirits rise,
Bathed in warmth beneath the skies.
With open hearts, we greet the morn,
In the light of love, we are reborn.

Beneath the Sky's Blushing Promise

Cotton clouds in blush attire,
Painted hues of soft desire.
A whisper trails through balmy air,
Dreams emerge without a care.

Gentle breezes brush the trees,
Nature's songs, a sweet reprise.
Nestled beneath this vast expanse,
Hearts embrace the morning dance.

Sunlight spills in tender rays,
Igniting hope in myriad ways.
Fields aglow with vibrant cheer,
Promise whispers, life is near.

In each corner, colors bloom,
Life awakens, dispelling gloom.
With every breath, a new start,
Nature's canvas, a work of art.

Underneath this dreamy haze,
We find joy in simple ways.
Together here, hand in hand,
Beneath the sky, a love so grand.

The Awakening Heartbeat of Day

A pulse of light breaks through the shade,
The world around anew displayed.
Soft whispers call, the night is done,
The heart of day has just begun.

Ticking clocks and rustling leaves,
Nature sighs, a web it weaves.
With every heartbeat, life takes shape,
In its rhythm, dreams escape.

Golden hues kiss the waking ground,
In every corner, life is found.
Awakening hearts, we rise and thrive,
In the morning glow, we come alive.

Hope dances lightly on each breeze,
Lifting spirits, calming unease.
As the sun peeks over the rise,
We heed the call, with joyful eyes.

Together we greet this tender dawn,
In the heartbeat of day, we are drawn.
With every pulse, the joy we share,
In the awakening, love is our prayer.

Beginnings in the Glow of Dawn

In morning's light, new paths are laid,
Destinies shaped, fears gently swayed.
Bright horizons greet our gaze,
The glow of dawn sets hearts ablaze.

Softly shines the warming sun,
From the shadows, we've now begun.
With each step on this fresh stage,
We turn the page, embrace the age.

Birds take flight in vivid arcs,
Chasing dreams, leaving marks.
A canvas bright with each new day,
Awakening souls in joyous play.

A tranquil breeze stirs the air,
Whispers of chance linger everywhere.
In the dawn's embrace, we find our truth,
Youthful spirits rejuvenate our youth.

As shadows yield to the sun's soft glow,
We unearth seeds of love to grow.
In the beginnings found at dawn,
Life's beauty, forever drawn.

The Canvas of Possibilities

On a barren field of dreams,
Colors begin to dance and sway,
Each hue a whisper of hope,
Painting futures bright and gay.

With strokes of courage and light,
We sketch our wishes in the air,
Boundless paths laid out before,
With every heartbeat, we dare.

Shades of joy and shadows of fear,
Blend together in our eyes,
Crafting stories yet untold,
Underneath the endless skies.

We hold the brush with steady hands,
Drawing dreams beyond the sun,
In this canvas, we find meaning,
A journey shared by everyone.

So let us paint with every breath,
A masterpiece of hope and light,
For within this vibrant canvas,
Lies the power to ignite.

Flight of Morning's Spirit

Awake the world with gentle sighs,
As dawn unveils her golden wings,
She carries dreams upon her back,
To where the softest sunlight sings.

The whispers of the waking trees,
Guide her flight across the skies,
With every flutter, she brings warmth,
And fills the air with sweet replies.

Dew-kissed petals greet her glance,
In hues of lavender and rose,
While shadows melt beneath her light,
In every corner, life bestows.

She spirals high through azure realms,
Enveloping the earth in grace,
Unlocking hearts, igniting hope,
In this celestial embrace.

As morning's spirit takes her flight,
Every moment gleams anew,
An orchestra of life unfolds,
With melodies that linger through.

Notes of Daybreak

The piano of dawn softly plays,
In whispers of a brand new day,
Each note a promise of release,
In every chord, our fears decay.

Rays of sunlight touch the keys,
Harmonies of warmth arise,
While echoes of the night depart,
Transforming dreams into the skies.

The breeze carries the sweetest tunes,
As flowers sway in gentle dance,
Nature joins in perfect rhythm,
In this awakening expanse.

With each note, the world expands,
New possibilities to chase,
In this symphony of daybreak,
We find our joy, our sacred space.

So close your eyes and listen well,
To the music of the morn,
For in these vibrant notes we find,
A universe, reborn.

Radiant Reassurance

In the darkest hour of night,
A glow emerges, soft and clear,
Radiant warmth wraps around hearts,
A gentle whisper, "I am near."

Stars twinkle like friendly eyes,
Guiding through the veil of doubt,
Each flicker a reminder of hope,
Where shadows are cast out.

With every heartbeat, light persists,
Shining through the cracks of pain,
In storms of sorrow, find your strength,
For sunshine will break through the rain.

Together we rise with courage,
Hand in hand, we face the day,
With radiant assurance glowing,
Chasing every fear away.

So let the light within us grow,
A beacon bright against the night,
In unity, we have the power,
To turn darkness into light.

Stirrings of Belief

In the quiet of the night, whispers rise,
Dreams take flight under starlit skies.
Hope ignites, a gentle flame,
Awakening hearts to love's sweet name.

Voices murmur soft and low,
Planting seeds where faith can grow.
With every dawn, a chance to mend,
The stirring belief that will not bend.

Each struggle faced, a lesson learned,
In every heart, a fire burned.
Through darkest times, we will prevail,
For belief transforms, it will not fail.

With every tear, a story spun,
A tapestry of hope begun.
United souls, we rise above,
In the stirrings of a boundless love.

Morning's First Kiss

As the sun breaks through the gray,
Morning whispers, chasing night away.
Golden rays on dew-soaked grass,
A tender moment, fleeting, alas.

Birds awaken, their songs afloat,
A symphony in nature's coat.
Gentle breezes touch the skin,
Morning's first kiss, a day to begin.

Shadows retreat, the world ignites,
With laughter and joy, the heart invites.
Every sunrise, a painted sky,
A promise renewed as hours fly.

In this moment, all feels right,
Hope reborn with morning light.
Embrace the day, let worries cease,
In morning's kiss, we find our peace.

Harmony of Light and Hope

In the realm where shadows dance,
Light emerges, given a chance.
Hope weaves through the darkest night,
A melody of pure delight.

Colors blend, a vibrant hue,
Painting dreams from old to new.
Hearts unite in steady flow,
In the harmony of light and hope.

Every whisper, every prayer,
Guides our souls with gentle care.
Together, we rise, hearts aglow,
In the harmony, our spirits grow.

Through every storm, we find our way,
With love as our compass, come what may.
In each heartbeat, the rhythm shows,
The harmony of light that glows.

Roots of New Beginnings

From the earth, we rise anew,
Roots entwined, strong and true.
Breaking ground, we seek the light,
In every struggle, hearts ignite.

With each season, growth appears,
Nurtured by our hopes and fears.
Branches stretch towards the sky,
From the depths, we learn to fly.

Every ending, a dawn reborn,
In the soil, new dreams are sworn.
We gather strength from what has passed,
Roots of beginnings, deep and vast.

Together, we stand hand in hand,
Building bridges across the land.
In every heartbeat, we find our song,
Roots of new beginnings, proud and strong.

The Warmth of New Horizons

The sun rises bright and bold,
Painting skies in hues of gold,
With warmth that kisses the earth,
Awakening life, bringing rebirth.

Fields bloom with flowers anew,
Colors vibrant, fresh as dew,
Soft breezes carry sweet delight,
Embracing dreams in morning light.

Mountains stand in silent grace,
Whispering tales of time and space,
Each step forward, a new embrace,
Guiding hearts to their destined place.

The horizon calls with a gentle sigh,
Inviting souls to spread and fly,
With every dawn, a chance to soar,
To chase the dreams we all adore.

In this moment, hope ignites,
Filling days with endless sights,
A journey starts with each new spark,
As we venture into the unknown dark.

Signals from the Sky

Stars shimmer in the velvet night,
Guiding lost souls with their light,
A cosmic dance of distant dreams,
Whispering secrets through moonbeams.

Clouds drift slow in soft embrace,
Holding wishes in their grace,
Lightning flickers, a sudden flare,
Nature's voice, a song so rare.

Winds carry tales from afar,
Echoes of love, a shining star,
The universe hums a gentle tune,
Cradling hopes beneath the moon.

In every storm, a message found,
Powerful truths in silence bound,
Rain falls softly, a tender kiss,
Nature's way of remaking bliss.

Listen closely to the night,
Signals flutter, a pure delight,
In the stillness, wisdom flows,
The sky shares secrets that nobody knows.

Glimmers of Hope

In the darkest hours, a light appears,
A flicker of hope, calming fears,
With every heartbeat, it grows anew,
A promise that dreams can still come true.

Through shadows long, we find our way,
Each step leads us to a brighter day,
Like stars that pierce the night's embrace,
Guiding us with their gentle grace.

The dawn awakens, spilling gold,
Stories of courage quietly told,
In moments tough, we stand our ground,
Glimmers of hope in love abound.

When storms rage and the skies turn gray,
Look to the light that guides our way,
For in each challenge, strength we find,
With glimmers of hope that bind.

To keep on dreaming, to never cease,
In every struggle, we seek our peace,
Together we rise, forever strong,
With glimmers of hope, we all belong.

Awakening Whispers

The morning breaks with gentle sighs,
Nature stirs, as daylight flies,
Birds sing softly, a sweet refrain,
Awakening whispers, soft like rain.

Leaves rustle in the cool, fresh air,
A symphony played without a care,
Bees buzz sweetly, collecting gold,
In every moment, life unfolds.

The earth awakens, vibrant and free,
Embracing all that's meant to be,
Every heartbeat, a sacred song,
Welcoming life, where we belong.

In the stillness, we hear the call,
Of dreams that rise, never to fall,
With every breath, the world anew,
Awakening whispers, strong and true.

A day unfolds, with stories untold,
With hope in our hearts, we break the mold,
Together we journey, hand in hand,
Awakening whispers across this land.

Trust in the Unfolding Day

In the light of dawn, we stand so still,
Hopes awaken, hearts begin to thrill.
Each moment whispers, gently unfolds,
Trust in the day, let your spirit be bold.

The sun peeks through, a warm embrace,
Shadows retreat, sorrow finds its place.
With every heartbeat, a chance to rise,
Trust in the day, see the endless skies.

Nature sings softly, a sweet refrain,
Let go of worries, release the pain.
In the light's embrace, we find our way,
Trust in the unfolding of the day.

Breezes carry dreams, whispers of fate,
Open your heart, it's never too late.
With every dawn, a new path to tread,
Trust in the journey, let courage be fed.

As hours pass on, the sun will shine,
With each breath taken, we intertwine.
In the rhythm of time, we learn to play,
Trust in the magic of the unfolding day.

Twilight's Departure

As the sun dips low, colors blend,
A moment of pause, as day meets its end.
Whispers of night begin to awake,
Twilight's magic, in shadows we take.

Stars gently shimmer, bright in the dark,
Filling the night with their luminous spark.
The sky wears a cloak of deepening hue,
While the moon climbs high, bidding adieu.

Memories linger of the day that was,
Golden moments held without a pause.
In twilight's embrace, we breathe deep sighs,
Knowing life dances in cycles and ties.

Each star a story, each breeze a song,
In the quiet of night, we all belong.
With twilight's departure, dreams take their flight,
Guided by starlight through the velvet night.

As shadows deepen, we are embraced,
In the arms of the night, our worries erased.
With hope in our hearts, the dawn will arise,
But for now, we cherish the twilight skies.

Dawn's Gentle Caress

Whispers of dawn creep soft as a sigh,
Painting the world with the light from on high.
Each beam a promise, each hue a new start,
Dawn's gentle caress, it warms every heart.

The dew-kissed petals glisten and gleam,
Awakening life from a slumbered dream.
Birds sing sweetly, time starts to flow,
In dawn's embrace, we begin to grow.

A canvas of colors, where shadows retreat,
Dancing with hope on the path of our feet.
With every sunrise, a chance to renew,
Dawn's gentle whisper, softly pulls through.

In the golden glow, our dreams take flight,
Each moment a treasure shining so bright.
With open arms, we welcome the day,
Dawn's gentle caress, guiding our way.

As hours unfold, may we never forget,
That each new dawn brings joy without regret.
Through pain and triumph, we'll dance and we'll sway,
In the soft morning light, come what may.

Expectation in Each Ray

Sunlight filters through the leaves so green,
Where hope is woven into every scene.
With each new ray, a promise unfurls,
Expectation dances in the hearts of the girls.

Golden horizons stretch wide and far,
In the light of the sun, we discover who we are.
Each moment glowing with possibility,
Expectation arises, wild and free.

Let dreams take flight on the wings of the breeze,
In the warmth of the day, we find our ease.
With laughter that sparkles, igniting our play,
Expectation leads us, lighting the way.

In the warmth of the sun, new visions appear,
Chasing the shadows, shedding the fear.
With courage ignited in every heartbeat,
Expectation blooms in each sunlit street.

As the day unfolds, we embrace each chance,
In the dance of the sun, we take our stance.
With hope as our guide, we venture and sway,
Expectation alive in each bright ray.